GEOMETRY
Looking Down on Monster Town

Based on the Math Monsters™ public television series, developed in cooperation with the National Council of Teachers of Mathematics (NCTM).

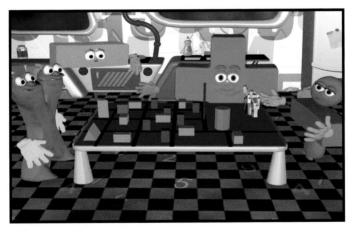

by John Burstein

Reading consultant: Susan Nations, M.Ed., author/literacy coach/consultant

Math curriculum consultants: Marti Wolfe, M.Ed., teacher/presenter; Kristi Hardi-Gilson, B.A., teacher/presenter

WEEKLY (WR) READER®
EARLY LEARNING LIBRARY

Please visit our web site at: **www.earlyliteracy.cc**
For a free color catalog describing Weekly Reader® Early Learning Library's list
of high-quality books, call 1-877-445-5824 (USA) or 1-800-387-3178 (Canada).
Weekly Reader® Early Learning Library's fax: (414) 336-0164.

Library of Congress Cataloging-in-Publication Data

Burstein, John.
   Geometry: looking down on Monster Town / by John Burstein.
     p. cm. — (Math monsters)
   Summary: The Math Monsters explain how things can look different depending
on one's perspective and explore the shapes of buildings in Monster Town.
   ISBN 0-8368-3809-2 (lib. bdg.)
   ISBN 0-8368-3824-6 (softcover)
   1. Geometry—Juvenile literature. [1. Shape. 2. Visual perception.] I. Title.
QA445.5.B88   2003
516—dc21
                                        2003045029

This edition first published in 2004 by
Weekly Reader® Early Learning Library
330 West Olive Street, Suite 100
Milwaukee, WI 53212 USA

Original Math Monsters™ animation: Destiny Images
Art direction, cover design, and page layout: Tammy Gruenewald
Editor: JoAnn Early Macken

Printed in the United States of America

1 2 3 4 5 6 7 8 9 07 06 05 04 03

You can enrich your children's mathematical experience by working
with them as they tackle the Corner Questions in this book. Create
a special notebook for recording their mathematical ideas.

Geometry and Math

By exploring two- and three-dimensional shapes, children gain
a greater understanding of geometry and a stronger sense
of spatial relationships.

Meet the
Math Monsters™

ADDISON

Addison thinks
math is fun.
"I solve problems
one by one."

Mina flies
from here to there.
"I look for answers
everywhere."

MINA

MULTIPLEX

Multiplex
sure loves to laugh.
"Both my heads
have fun with math."

Split is friendly
as can be.
"If you need help,
then count on me."

SPLIT

We're glad you want to take a look
at the story in our book.

We know that as you read, you'll see
just how helpful math can be.

Let's get started. Jump right in!
Turn the page, and let's begin!

The Math Monsters were up on the roof of their castle. They looked down on Monster Town. They felt so happy that they sang a song.

"It is fun to be looking down
at all the buildings in our town
and seeing what shapes can be found
in dear old Monster Town."

"I see lots of rectangles," said Multiplex.

"I see a triangle," said Split.

"The buildings look so small," said Mina. "Some of them look even smaller than the birdhouse right here on our roof."

"How can that be?" asked Addison. "We have all been in the buildings in town. None of us can fit in this birdhouse."

Why do you think the buildings look smaller than the birdhouse?

"I think the buildings look smaller because they are far away," said Split. "The birdhouse looks bigger because it is close to us."

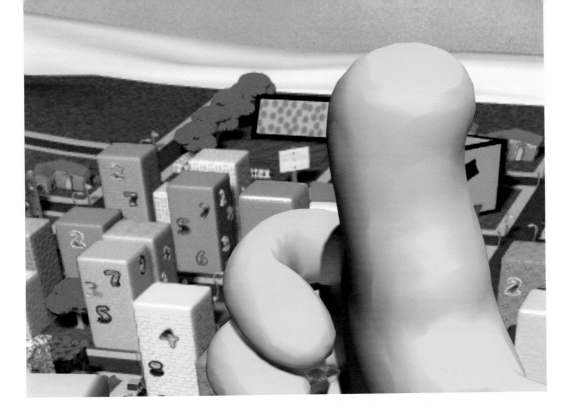

"That is just like my thumb," said Multiplex. "When I hold it close to my eyes, it looks much bigger than the buildings. I know it is really not."

"Let's go to town and see how big the buildings really are," said Addison.

When you get closer to a building, does it look bigger or smaller?

Their first stop was Aunt Two Lips' Garden Shop.

"It looks a lot bigger now that we are close to it," said Multiplex. He made up a little song.

"I look at something far away,
and it seems much smaller,
but as I move in closer,
it looks bigger and much taller.
I know it does not change its size,
but it really fools my eyes."

"Let's draw the shapes we see," said Split. "I will draw the front."

"I will draw one side," said Multiplex.

"I will draw the other side," said Addison.

"I will draw the back," said Mina.

What shapes do you think the monsters will draw?

"I drew a triangle for the front," said Split.

"I drew a rectangle for one side," said Multiplex.

"I drew a rectangle for the other side," said Addison.

"I drew a triangle for the back," said Mina.

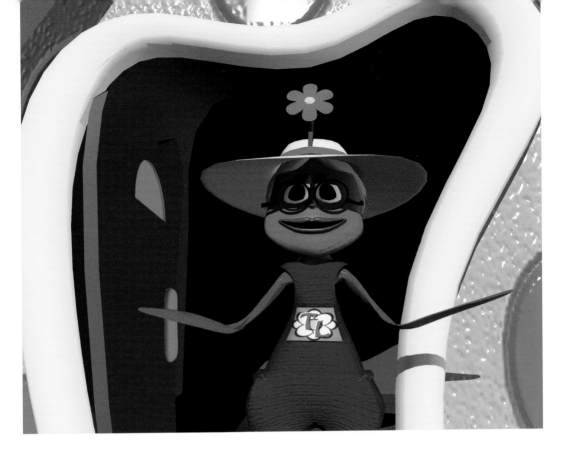

Aunt Two Lips opened her door.
She said, "Can you guess the shape
of my floor?"

*Do you think the
monsters will
guess a triangle
or a rectangle?*

Aunt Two Lips used monster magic to make the walls of her shop fade away.

"Your floor has the shape of a rectangle," said Mina.

"That is right," said Aunt Two Lips. "My shop is made with two triangles and three rectangles."

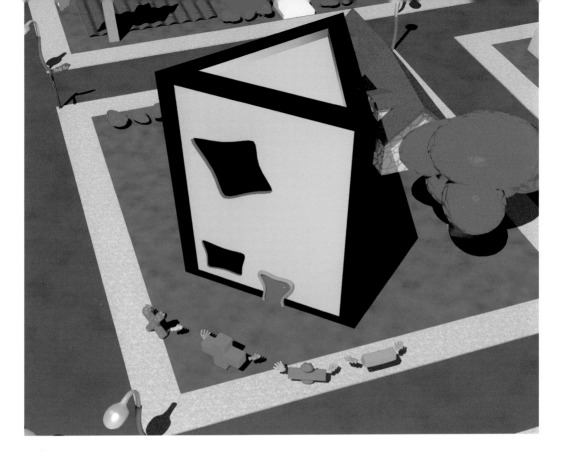

The monsters went to see Cousin Digit's house.

"Let's draw the shapes we see," said Split.

What shapes do you think the monsters will draw?

Mina flew up to the roof. She drew a triangle.

Split, Addison, and Multiplex each drew a rectangle
for the walls.

"That makes one triangle
and three rectangles," said Split.
"I wonder what shape the floor is."

*What shape
do you think
the floor is?*

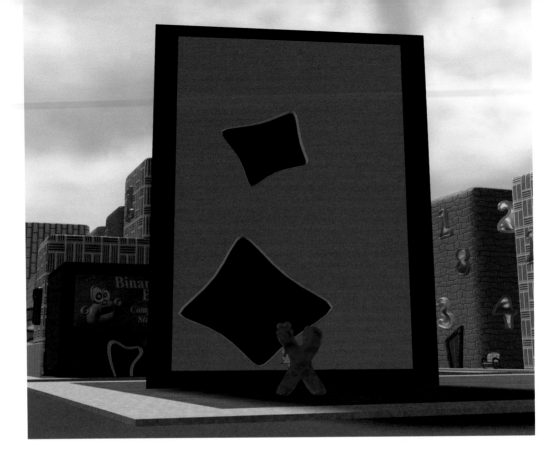

Multiplex looked in the window. He said, "The floor is a triangle just like the roof."

"This building is made with two triangles and three rectangles," said Addison.

"Those are the shapes we just drew for Aunt Two Lips' shop," said Multiplex.

"How can that be?" asked Mina. "They look so different!"

The two buildings are made with the same shapes. Why do they look different?

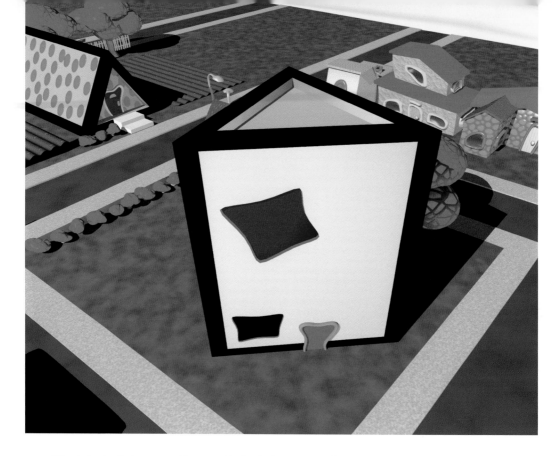

"I think I know," said Addison. "If we use our minds, we can pretend to tip Cousin Digit's house onto its side. When we do that, it will look like Aunt Two Lips' shop."

"We can also pretend to tip Aunt Two Lips' shop onto its front," said Split. "It will look the same as Cousin Digit's house."

The monsters went to Big Bill's Computer Store.

"These two sides are squares," said Multiplex.

"The roof is also a square," said Mina.

Will the shape of the other walls and floor be squares or circles?

Big Bill came out. He said, "The other walls and the floor are all squares. My shop has six sides: four walls, a roof, and a floor. They are all squares. That makes my shop a cube."

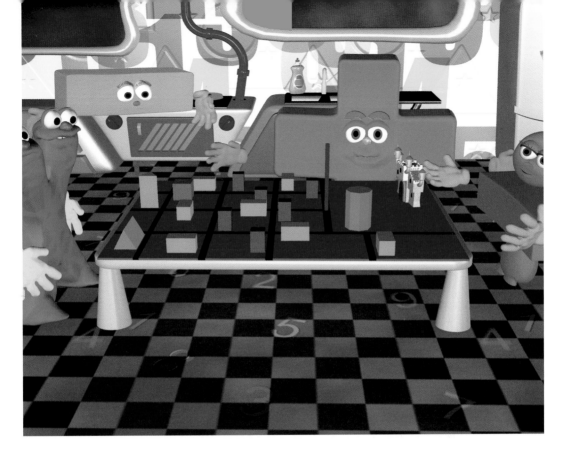

All day, the monsters looked at the buildings of Monster Town. Then they went home. They built a model of Monster Town with blocks.

Do you like building with blocks? What do you notice about their shapes and sides?

Addison picked up two blocks. First he showed
Split the ends. Then he turned them to show the sides.
"Wow!" said Split. "Let me try that."

Split picked up two more blocks. She did the same thing.

"Shapes can be so much fun to learn about," she said.

The monsters worked on their model. They sang,

"Rectangles, triangles,
circles round
are shapes we found
in Monster Town."

When you take a walk around your neighborhood, what shapes do you see?

ACTIVITIES

Page 5 Take two paper plates of equal size. Place one close by and the other far away across the room. Talk about which plate looks bigger and why.

Page 7 Have children look at an object that is far away, such as a car, a tree, or the moon. Ask each child to close one eye and hold up his or her thumb in front of the other eye. Watch the children have fun making objects disappear behind their thumbs.

Pages 9, 11, 13, 15, 17 Using construction paper, create a model of Aunt Two Lips' shop and a model of Cousin Digit's house. The formal name for this geometric shape made with three rectangles and two triangles is "triangular prism." Use the models you make to help children investigate the concepts on these pages. Have fun decorating the buildings.

Page 19 Children can use dice or blocks to explore the properties of cubes. They may need your help to be sure each side is only counted once.

Page 21 Encourage children to count the sides and name the shapes of a variety of building blocks. Discuss similarities and differences between models and real objects such as toy cars, trucks, or dollhouses.

Page 23 This is a great time for a walk around the neighborhood. Ask children what shapes they notice. See if they can spot two- and three-dimensional geometric shapes. Cut out pictures of buildings with interesting shapes and make a geometric collage.